A FIELD GUIDE TO WEDDING GUESTS

HELEN REID

First published 2021 by Poet's House Pamphlets,
Oxford, 14 Kineton Road, Oxford OX1 4PG
poetshousepamphlets.co.uk

Designed by Frances Kiernan
www.franceskiernan.co.uk

Printed by Dalton Printers, Cardiff.
www.daltonprinters.co.uk

ISBN 978-1-7399748-0-0

For Frankie, Tom and Hugo

Acknowledgements

The following poems previously appeared in IOTA Magazine:
'The First Wife's Skin Cells', 'Breaking' and 'Homecoming'.

The following were prize-winning poems appearing in
The Blue Nib Chapbook 6: 'Press this Shell to your Ear',
'The Suburban Ornithologist', 'The Ceilidh', 'Wedding Algae'
and 'The Sullen Infanta'.

I would like to thank Jenny Lewis for her unwavering support
for this project and for her guidance and wisdom in my
unfolding as a poet; Frances Kiernan for the beautiful design
of this pamphlet, and my friends, family and particularly my
fellow poets, Catherine Faulds, Margot Myers and Lyn
Thornton, for their encouragement.

Contents

A Field Guide to Wedding Guests

1: The Sullen Infanta

A tiny girl is a central point in the flurry
of shuffling on the church steps.
She stands bleakly in a pearl-studded bodice,
obediently holding her skirt out at both sides,
posies of artificial mock orange bound to her wrists
and pinned firmly into her tiara.

If the photo is taken now, she will be
the only thing in focus. Those glum eyes
will be destined to follow the happy couple
round every living room they ever share.
They will look at her and wonder
if she knew then what they know now.

The First Wife's Skin Cells

He made this wooden bed for you and him,
romancing your poverty. Pride seeps
from the structure. Spring sap. I have built
my fine nest high. New stains map the mattress
where my waters broke. Yet beneath me
your skin cells cluster in the joints,
settle deep in the grain where discarded hair
burrows the cracks of a creaking frame,
calibrated by your rhythm. I listen
to ancestors of dust mites fattened
on the stuff of your sediment and sweat.
I could clone you from this bed,
resurrect you just to prove that it is me
he wants. That is why I do not let him burn it.

Breaking

Breaking news: a woman's let her tea go cold.
A bulletin. She weeps. Do we have sound?
And the family of the soldier has been told.

It's official. Of the hundred who were polled
ninety five percent agree she should be proud.
Back to the scene. Yes, the woman's tea's still cold.

We will keep you posted as events unfold.
Now the weather. In the flooding all hopes drowned
for the family of the soldier who've been told.

We've just heard that he was twenty-one years old.
It's so tragic; next the value of the pound.
Join our phone in. What's your take on tea gone cold?

Now the virtue of the boy must be extolled,
for his body, even now, is homeward bound
to the family of the soldier who've been told.

Just to recap then, with him they broke the mould.
Though his blood's still warm in distant desert ground
yet our experts can confirm her tea is cold
and the family of the soldier has been told.

A Field Guide to Wedding Guests

2: Bitch

The man to my left has been itching
to show me a snap of his dog. He strikes
between courses to pull out his pin-up
which he passes to me, with a radiant smile
and also a strange spitty sound,
which might be the name of the breed
or of just this one creature,
sprawled on a deep-pile red carpet,
exposed, shameless, content.
While I could be anyone.

A Field Guide to Wedding Guests

3: Wedding Algae

We're all just an algal bloom,
he explains, *and a rapid expansion in numbers*
like this will result in, and he pauses to slice
through his lamb, *a dead sea.*
Is there no hope at all,
I enquire, but he swallows my question,
with a glug of the red, and cheerfully waves,
at his tiny doomed sons, who with dozens
of other small children, are swarming around
the sad slow dissolve of two love birds of ice.

Sonnet to an Urban Fox

Meet me, old lover, on the hill tonight
share a view of the city spread wide.
I'll point out the landmarks, the places we made
snap decisions, promises, fatal mistakes.
Breathe in the reek of its perfume and piss,
past its best, but better than anything since.
Hold me close on the hill while the city lights up,
more defined in the darkness, more sure of its map.

Join me to scavenge for thrills and delights
to sniff out old dreams in the pavement cracks
round the back of the cafes and clubs.
Join me and the blackbirds to sing through the night,
baring our souls to the drunks and the rats,
in the jaundice of streetlamps and cabs.

A Field Guide to Wedding Guests

4: The Ceilidh

Two abstainers sit on hard plastic chairs,
backs to the buffet table, as the dancers couple up.
The woman on the left finds herself

back in the rancid school gymnasium
where every Tuesday she was made to dance
with partially-pubesced Scottish boys,

the tops of whose oily heads would only just reach
her statuesque Anglo-Saxon chest,
so that she had almost to bend double

for the birling bit of the Gay Gordons,
which, she imagined, with the right partner,
might have been a joyous release.

The man to her right is tapping his collapsible
walking stick to the Dashing White Sergeant.
Time was, he'd peel the two meekest-looking lassies

away from the safety of the wall, to frame him,
take each by a pastel cardigan-clad arm
and, like a lad on a fairground waltzer,

whirl them round so hard and fast
that their skirts would billow up
and they'd scream as their feet left the floor.

The Suburban Ornithologist

Heron, Osney Bridge

    Still, in the archway
    knee cocked, Cleopatra eyes,
    she is poised to strike.

The Charm

    A flock of dandies
    studs the newly budded ash,
    bright with diamond song.

Oatlands Road

    Pigeons are mating
    on the TV aerial
    during peak viewing.

The Suburban Ornithologist

The Botley Road

Screech of swifts cutting
through hopeful smoke signals
from English barbecues.

Modesty

By the path, unseen
a living leaf waits.
The unassuming dunnock.

Flood Flowers

Black headed gulls bloom
on the wildflower meadow.
First flood of winter.

Bleak

Midwinter morning,
the birdbath has frozen.
Indignant robin.

Angel

So, bored of being guide and guardian, I let him take the lead,
down to his yeasty lair, a basement room, just off the Balls
Pond Road and while I cast off pearls and plumage, slipped off
silken robes, he strained in socks on tippy toes to suck my neck,
my chin, my glacial lobes. He really grunted loads, as both
hands worried at the fastenings of my jewel-encrusted
underclothes. He closed both dazzled mammal eyes, and took a
running jump to fell me to his bed. I let him root around on top
until the static from his nylon sheets gave me a charge, went to
my head. I set to work on him instead, I did, that lucky little
hominid, whose earth was moved within a general realignment
of the stars in Islington that night. I left him there, punching the
air I flew through.

A Field Guide to Wedding Guests

5: Sister of the Bride, Portrait

Beyond the Function Suite, there is a garden
where the smokers and the weary can retreat.
The older sister of the bride,
barefoot and alone, chignon undone,
leans against the back wall,
framed by the discarded bridal arch
which has developed a list to the left.

Despite some sort of pap still caked on her dress,
she's no longer the baby-draped drudge
overlooked by all throughout the day.
Aware of occasional glances
from the huddle of lads by the door,
she inhales serenely from her roll-up,
blows little smoke haloes up to the sky.

A child cries out her name into the dark
and she shrugs, glides back across the grass,
stooping here and there
to retrieve her kicked-off slingbacks,
passing the humanist celebrant
who is rushing towards a Cinquecento
parked nearby for a quick escape.

A Field Guide to Wedding Guests:

6: Mr Tongue

It was the seventies, and we were swigging cider
straight from a bottle we'd nicked from the bar.
He found us on the hotel staircase, me behind Ange
so others could pass us, go up to their rooms,
or back down to the dance.

At seventeen, we thought we had to play along
to keep the peace and giggle at the menace in his jokes.
I answered any questions with as few words as I could,
tracking the lit cigar he dangled too close to my neck
from his yellowed fingers.

Unsteady now, he leaned right in, the kiss goodbye,
and more resigned than me, Ange offered up a cheek.
Of course he wanted only mouth. She rolled her eyes
and pulled a face, but I shrank back, and turned away
No thank you. I don't want a kiss.

He hissed some words, as he staggered off,
Your eyes are too clever, he spat, *too clever by far,*
he missed the last stair but remained on his feet,
brayed to his pals at the bar while Ange wiped her mouth
and sighed, *he slipped the tongue.*

When the bottle was empty and Ange had been sick
we rejoined the grown-ups and there he was,
someone's uncle in the disco dance, working the room,
and though I was too clever then, all I could do
was make fun of his wife.

Press this Shell to your Ear

I met him on a northern winter shore, my silkie boy,
his slippery kiss, it blanched my swollen lips
with brine. By early spring, my skin was cracked
and wafer flakes broke off as he stroked
the blisters on my upturned face.
Such brittle clumps dropped each time
he ran his fingers through my once fine hair
that even he could see that I was sick
with missing salt-free streams and meadow dew.
So he and I drove south through hedgerows
green with fresh growth, flushed with budding.

All the way he kept up such a sea pup keening,
I had to toss a mermaid's purse for him to chew,
clamp a cowrie to his ear to make him sleep.
I dug a pond deep in my orchard where each pink dawn
he stripped down to his oily grey hide,
lay mournful in his landlocked pit of mud.
We nailed a tidal clock to the ceiling above our bed
to mark the highs and lows, until the day
I woke up in a sweet dry bed and found the cowrie
on his pillow, so that now and then, on a stormy night,
or a spring tide, I still can share his distant rushing joy.

Waiting Room in Lanarkshire

i

This was our teenage air-lock,
the space between
chintz and the city,
our shabby strobe-lit boudoir,
for the hitch up of skirts,
the smudging of lids,
the frosting of pouts.

ii

I remember when sleet
could drive us inside.
From the huddle, a hand
would reach up to pull the cord
of the one-bar electric heater
and our heads would tilt as one,
suburban sunflowers,
towards our rationed heat
which switched itself off
every two minutes.

Waiting Room in Lanarkshire

iii

Just for a while,
my father sits
engine running,
gloved fingers
tapping the wheel.
I raise a hand
to wave through glass
and he's off with a nod,
in the small white car
up Station Road.
Will these be the last glimpses?
Just before he turns
it comes, the jaunty toot.

Homecoming

Even so, I stay at the guest house where
in an atmosphere thick with other souls
and brassica, I lie on a single mattress made
slippery with plastic protection, in a room
with a view of the dawn or the dusk painted
by numbers, nailed to the wall, hung over
my head. Though a room lies empty elsewhere,
here are ornaments to wonder at: a bowl
of dust and dead buds freshened up by a spray,
peach perhaps; a grimy shepherdess standing dainty
guard over teabags and powdered milk in Tupperware.
And when the dawn chorus of expanding pipes reaches
its thermostatic climax, I will send out a signal,
a teaspoon, tapped, repeated, on the radiator.

A Field Guide to Wedding Guests

7: The Distant Cousin

She arrives all in black, after dark
for the evening do only.
She's Theda Bara in lycra,
ashen-faced with raven eyes
scanning the floor, ranking the hapless,
the ushers, first cousins
and friends of the groom from work.

In the reeking clash of perfumes
of the powder room our paths cross
in front of the slap-splattered mirror.
She does not see me
or my disappointment
that she casts a reflection next to mine,
as she wipes lipstick off her canines.

Opus Criminale

On learning that the mosaic floor of the
Museum of Childhood, Bethnal Green,
was made by women prisoners.

Now all I can see is a scheme of squares
within squares, on a board over which
children skip while glass-eyed dolls
look on. Each small part of this stone quilt
a testament to desperation, the submission of
wantons, the stoical fingers of souls
once contained by Woking Gaol.

Regular pieces of work lie next to
rebellious crammings of jagged tile.
Cell by cell by row this opus criminale
stretches out, revealing the pattern,
while the offspring of the well-read
scrabble through the gift shop
in search of something cheap.

A Field Guide to Wedding Guests

8: The Extra

No one likes to look, but in this otherwise
immaculate production, a young woman in powder blue

who had been hurriedly ushered from the dance
has re-emerged to loom tragically by the buffet

from which she periodically picks at abandoned
sprigs of parsley and lets her abundant eye make-up

slide down a face so blackened now that
she resembles someone who has wandered in

from the wrong film set where she'd fled
a burning building only to stand in the rain.

A Field Guide to Wedding Guests

9: The Great Aunt

She drops off
and takes on
scraps of news,
staggers to every table,
on legs like
Twiglets in court shoes.